JOIE WARNER'S SPAGHETTI

joie warner's

spaghetti

america's favorite pasta

DESIGNED AND PHOTOGRAPHED BY

DREW WARNER

HEARST BOOKS
New York

a

flavor

book

It is the policy of William Morrow and Company, Inc. and its
imprints and affiliates, recognizing the importance of preserving
what has been written, to print the books we publish on acid-free
paper, and we exert our best efforts to that end.

Library of Congress Cataloging-in-Publication Data
Warner, Joie.
[Spaghetti]
Joie Warner's spaghetti: America's favorite pasta /
by Joie Warner; photographs by Drew Warner.
p.   cm.
ISBN 0-688-12808-4
1. Cookery (Pasta)   I. Title.   II. Title: Spaghetti.
TX809.M17W347   1994
641.8'22—dc20   93-41263
CIP
Printed in Singapore   10 9 8 7 6 5 4 3 2 1

This book was created and produced by
Flavor Publications, Inc.
208 East 51st Street, Suite 240
New York, New York 10022

FIRST EDITION

ACKNOWLEDGMENTS

MY LOVE AND APPRECIATION to my husband Drew, agent, producer, designer, and photographer extraordinaire. This and all my other books could not have been done without him. My thanks also go to Margaret Jackson for her editorial skills, and a big thank you to the wonderful people at William Morrow.

C O N T E N T S

EVERYONE LOVES
spaghetti. And it's no wonder. The long, thin strands
are not only fun to slurp but they are delightfully
deliciously delectable! What's more, spaghetti is easy to
buy, incredibly cheap, and simplicity itself to prepare.

Spaghetti is a classic—it's the first pasta
everyone thinks of. Always there on the pantry shelf,
it's perfectly designed for spur-of-the-moment meals.
As well, spaghetti is superbly suited to any occasion
from the fanciest dinner to the simplest family supper.
And no other pasta shape can be prepared in so many
ways—fried for nibbles, simmered in soups, tumbled
with cooked or uncooked sauces, tossed in salads,
baked in casseroles—and even served up for dessert.

But perhaps its real appeal in the '90s is that this
satisfying staple is so healthy and versatile. Loaded with
complex carbohydrates and low in calories and fat,
spaghetti can be sauced in myriad ways using good-for-
you olive oil—instead of butter—and fresh produce

and no—or very little—meat. You'll notice that none of my main-course recipes contains meat or heavy cream (you'll never miss it!), and the majority are centered around the season's freshest vegetables and herbs. But the truth is, I've created these full-flavored recipes for people who—like me—love to eat. And the fact that most dishes are as nutritious as they are delicious is just a terrific bonus.

All of my recipes are exceedingly easy and speedy to prepare—I favor zesty, colorful sauces that don't need cooking or, at the very most, can be made in the time it takes to boil the spaghetti.

But before you begin, here are a few tips on preparation. Always start with the best and freshest ingredients you can find. Purchase spaghetti made with 100 percent durum semolina (all the recipes in this book are for dried spaghetti) and always cook it in plenty of rapidly boiling salted water—at least five quarts of water to one pound of pasta. Don't add the salt (about one to two tablespoons) until the water has come to a full boil and never add oil to the water or the sauce won't cling to the pasta. Add spaghetti, stirring constantly to prevent the strands from sticking together, and cover the pot until the water returns to the boil. Remove the lid, then place it on halfway to maintain a rapid boil. Continue stirring occasionally while it cooks, and after about four minutes begin

testing for doneness by removing a strand and biting into it. Continue this testing process every minute or so until just a tiny white core remains in the center and the texture is *al dente*, that is, tender yet slightly firm.

The instant the spaghetti is done, drain it in a colander, or use one of those special spaghetti forks. Gently shake to remove excess water but don't overdo it—a little moisture is necessary or the resulting dish could turn out dry. And don't rinse drained spaghetti or toss with olive oil unless the recipe specifies. It is also a good idea to retain a little of the spaghetti water in case the sauce needs a bit more moisture. Working quickly, transfer the spaghetti to the sauce and toss, using two forks, until thoroughly combined, then transfer again to a warmed shallow serving bowl or platter, or warmed dinner plates (unless the dish, of course, is to be served cold or at room temperature). Serve steaming hot spaghetti with a tossed green salad, some crusty bread—and perhaps a glass of wine—for a meal that is as delicious and simple as can be.

Finally, for those still wondering whether to use a spoon to help gather up the long strands onto a fork, the answer is this: the experts at eating spaghetti—the Italians, of course—never use a spoon and neither should you. The correct way to eat spaghetti is to lift a small amount of spaghetti and sauce onto your fork, then twirl the fork around a few times until the noodles form a fairly neat bundle with just a few strands hanging loose. You may twirl with the fork resting against the side of the bowl or plate—but never ever cut spaghetti—it was designed to be twirled and enjoyed with gusto.

Having said all that, it's now time to join me in the kitchen. I do hope you'll discover many exciting new tastes and new ways to prepare this familiar old favorite and, above all, have as much fun playing with the recipes as I did creating them.

JOIE WARNER

SPAGHETTI CRISPS

*d*eep-fried spaghetti crisps are crunchy companions to preprandial drinks, burgers or sandwiches, and fun to use as a garnish.

  2 teaspoons salt
  ½ teaspoon cayenne
      About 4 tablespoons freshly grated Parmesan cheese
  8 ounces spaghettini
  1 teaspoon olive oil
      About 3 cups vegetable oil

Mix salt and cayenne in small bowl, place cheese in another; set both aside. ∾ Cook pasta in large pot of boiling salted water until *al dente*. Drain very well or oil will spatter when frying. Toss with olive oil to prevent pasta from sticking together. ∾ Using scissors, cut spaghetti into roughly 2- to 4-inch lengths; set on tray beside stove. Heat vegetable oil to 350°F in wok or deep-fryer (and maintain correct heat throughout cooking or crisps will be oily). Fry pasta in several batches—do not overcrowd pan or it won't be crisp (and turn only when sizzling begins to subside) until golden brown and crisp. As each batch is completed, remove with slotted spoon and drain on paper towels; immediately sprinkle with a little salt mixture, then cheese. Break up clumps into smaller pieces when cooled.

MAKES ABOUT 6 CUPS.

SPAGHETTI MINESTRONE

any minestrones take forever to cook and are often so thick you can stand a spoon up in them. My light-and-quick version joins together garden-fresh vegetables and long, thin spaghetti noodles—instead of the traditional tubular-shaped macaroni. Enjoy this dinner-in-a-bowl with some crusty Italian bread and a glass of wine. You may want to provide a fork along with the soup spoon for ease of eating, or break the pasta into halves or thirds before adding to the stockpot.

    2 tablespoons olive oil

    2 medium onions, chopped

    4 large garlic cloves, finely chopped

    2 medium carrots, chopped

    1 stalk celery, finely chopped

    2 quarts chicken stock

    1 quart water

    1 pound ripe plum or cherry tomatoes, coarsely chopped

  ½ pound vermicelli

    1 medium zucchini (½ pound), unpeeled, cut into julienne

    1 medium yellow summer squash (½ pound), unpeeled, cut into julienne

    1 can (14 ounces) white kidney beans, drained

    1 tablespoon dried basil
       Salt and freshly ground black pepper

  ½ cup freshly grated Parmesan cheese, plus extra for serving

    1 cup coarsely chopped fresh basil leaves

Heat oil in large nonstick skillet over medium heat. Add onions, garlic, carrots, and celery; cook for 10 minutes or until vegetables are just tender. Transfer to large stockpot and add chicken stock and water; bring to a simmer. Add tomatoes and cook for 20 minutes. Bring to a boil; add pasta and cook for 5 minutes, stirring frequently to prevent pasta from sticking together. Add zucchini, yellow summer squash, kidney beans, dried basil, salt, and pepper; cook another 5 minutes or just until vegetables are crisp-tender. Stir in cheese and basil. Serve with extra cheese and pass the peppermill.

SERVES 10.

SPAGHETTI WITH UNCOOKED
SMOKED SALMON, CAPERS,
AND DILL

moked salmon, fresh dill, red onion, and capers create an elegantly simple sauce for spaghetti. This enchanting entrée is a terrific choice for a special occasion. Italians would never suggest serving cheese with fish, but I'm not Italian, so I can break the rules!

6 ounces thinly sliced smoked salmon, very coarsely chopped
¼ cup plus 2 tablespoons olive oil
2 large garlic cloves, finely chopped
1 generous tablespoon drained tiny capers
¼ cup coarsely chopped fresh dill
Freshly ground black pepper
2 tablespoons freshly grated Parmesan cheese, plus extra for serving
½ pound spaghetti or vermicelli
¼ cup diced red onion

Place smoked salmon—separating pieces that clump together—in large serving bowl. Gently stir in oil, garlic, capers, dill, pepper, and cheese. ꙮ Cook pasta in large pot of boiling salted water until *al dente*. Drain well and add to salmon mixture. Toss until combined. Sprinkle with onion and serve with extra cheese.

SERVES 3 TO 4.

SPAGHETTI WITH GOAT CHEESE, TOMATOES, AND BASIL

oat cheese, tomatoes, and basil make one of the loveliest, creamiest sauces (without the addition of heavy, high-fat cream) for spaghetti, with the added bonus that it takes merely minutes to make.

¼ cup olive oil
2 large garlic cloves, finely chopped
¾ pound ripe cherry tomatoes, quartered
Salt and freshly ground black pepper
½ pound spaghetti
½ cup coarsely chopped fresh basil or flat-leaf parsley, plus extra for garnish
2 ounces soft, mild goat cheese, coarsely crumbled

Heat oil in large nonstick skillet over medium-high heat. Add garlic and cook for 1 minute or until tender. Add tomatoes, salt, and pepper and cook for 2 minutes or until heated through but still holding their shape; keep warm. ❧ Meanwhile, cook pasta in large pot of boiling salted water until *al dente*. Drain well and add to sauce in skillet. Sprinkle with basil and toss to combine. Sprinkle with goat cheese and toss lightly until partially combined; don't overmix. Transfer to large serving bowl; garnish with basil and pass the peppermill.

SERVES 2 TO 3.

SPAGHETTI WITH PESTO SAUCE IN TOMATOES

t hese *funky-looking tomatoes stuffed with basil-laced spaghetti make an especially charming first course or luncheon entrée. Serve either at room temperature, or bake and serve hot. Flavorful tomatoes are essential.*

- 6 to 8 large ripe tomatoes
- 3 large garlic cloves
- 2 cups lightly packed fresh basil leaves
- ¼ cup pecan halves, lightly toasted
- ½ cup olive oil
- ½ cup freshly grated Parmesan cheese
- ½ pound spaghetti
  Salt and freshly ground black pepper

Slice off tops (about ¼ inch) of tomatoes and scoop out seeds and pulp leaving ¼-inch shell. Drain tomatoes cut side down on paper towels. ❧ Finely chop garlic, basil, and pecans in food processor—not to a paste. With machine running, add oil in thin stream until smooth. Add cheese and blend. ❧ Cook pasta in large pot of boiling salted water until *al dente*. Drain well and place in large bowl. Add pesto sauce and sprinkle with salt and pepper; toss until combined. Fill tomatoes with equal amounts of pasta and serve at room temperature or place in baking dish and bake in preheated 400°F oven for 15 minutes or just until heated through.

SERVES 6 TO 8.

photo overleaf 👉

SPAGHETTI WITH UNCOOKED
ORANGE-FLAVORED TOMATO SAUCE

a wonderfully vibrant sauce embellished with sweet fragrant basil and the tart contrast of orange zest. The preparation couldn't be easier—or the aroma more intoxicating—simply combine the ingredients, then set aside awhile before tossing with cooked pasta.

3 large garlic cloves, finely chopped
  Grated zest of 1 large orange
2 pounds ripe tomatoes, seeded, coarsely chopped
¾ cup coarsely shredded fresh basil leaves
½ teaspoon dried thyme
¼ teaspoon cayenne
¼ cup freshly grated Parmesan cheese, plus extra for
  serving
⅓ cup olive oil
  Salt and freshly ground black pepper
¾ pound spaghetti

Combine garlic, orange zest, tomatoes, half the basil, thyme, cayenne, cheese, oil, salt, and pepper in large mixing bowl. Set aside for 1 to 2 hours—no longer—to allow flavors to blend, stirring occasionally. ❧ Cook pasta in large pot of boiling salted water until al dente. Drain well, immediately toss with sauce mixture and transfer to platter or large serving bowl. Sprinkle with remaining basil and serve at once. Serve with extra cheese and pass the peppermill.

SERVES 4.

CURRIED SPAGHETTI SALAD

urry infuses spaghetti with its vivacious color and captivating fragrance. Sweet shrimp, the tang of lime, and the fresh garden flavor of red peppers, scallions, and basil add beautiful contrast. My recipe was inspired by one in the David Wood Food Book.

¾ pound spaghettini or vermicelli, broken in half
¼ cup olive oil
2 large garlic cloves, finely chopped
¼ teaspoon hot red pepper flakes (optional)
2 tablespoons best-quality curry powder
2 tablespoons oyster sauce
1 pound cooked small shrimp
   Grated zest of 1 medium lime
2 tablespoons fresh lime juice
1 sweet red pepper, seeded, cut into fine julienne
4 green onions (green part only), finely shredded
1 cup coarsely shredded fresh basil leaves
1 teaspoon sugar
½ teaspoon salt

Cook pasta in large pot of boiling salted water until *al dente*. Drain and rinse under cold running water; drain again. ∾ Heat oil in small skillet over medium-high heat. Add garlic and red pepper flakes; cook for 30 seconds. Add curry powder; cook for 1 minute and remove from heat. Stir in oyster sauce. ∾ Toss curry mixture with pasta in very large bowl until evenly distributed. Add remaining ingredients; toss again.

SERVES 6 TO 8.

SPAGHETTI WITH SWEET RED
PEPPER SAUCE

*W*henever I serve this, my guests always think it's
*spaghetti with tomato sauce—then they are delighted
to discover that red bell peppers are the secret behind the beguiling
sweetness of the sauce.*

- 1 tablespoon olive oil
- 1 tablespoon butter
- 3 large garlic cloves, chopped
- 1 cup chopped red onion
- 3 sweet red peppers (1¼ pounds), seeded, chopped
- 1⅓ cups chicken stock
  Salt and freshly ground black pepper
- ¾ pound spaghetti or spaghettini
- ½ cup chopped fresh basil or parsley, plus extra
  for garnish
  Grated zest of 1 medium-large lemon
  Freshly grated Parmesan cheese

Heat oil and butter in large nonstick skillet over medium-high
heat. Add garlic, onion, and red peppers and cook for 5 minutes
or until tender. Add chicken stock, salt, and pepper. Cover,
reduce heat, and simmer for 10 minutes or until vegetables are
very tender. Purée in food processor, return to pan, and simmer
for 8 minutes or until sauce thickens. ❧ Cook pasta in large pot
of boiling salted water until *al dente*. Drain well and add to sauce
in skillet. Sprinkle with basil; toss for 1 minute to allow pasta to
absorb flavors. Transfer to large serving bowl and sprinkle with
lemon zest. Serve with cheese and pass the peppermill.

SERVES 4.

SPAGHETTI EGGPLANT SANDWICHES

S *uch fun to make—even more fun to eat!*

2 eggplants (1 pound each), unpeeled
Salt
Olive oil
½ cup ricotta cheese
¼ cup freshly grated Parmesan cheese
¼ cup (½ stick) butter, melted
1 large ripe plum tomato, seeded, chopped
1 tablespoon chopped fresh basil leaves
Salt and freshly ground black pepper
6 ounces spaghetti
Several thin slices mozzarella cheese
1 large ripe plum tomato, thinly sliced
Basil leaves for garnish

Slice and remove ends of eggplants. Cut four ½-inch thick slices
from widest part of each eggplant, reserving the rest for another
use. Sprinkle both sides of slices with salt and set in large
colander in sink to drain for 1 hour. Pat slices dry with paper
towels. ॐ Preheat grill or broiler. Brush both sides of eggplant
slices with oil and place on grill or broiling rack. Grill for
2 minutes, then turn, and cook another 2 minutes or just until
cooked through; set aside. ॐ Combine ricotta, Parmesan cheese,
butter, tomato, basil, salt, and pepper in large bowl. Cook pasta
in large pot of boiling salted water until *al dente*. Drain well and
toss with ricotta mixture. ॐ Place 4 of the largest eggplant slices
in single layer on lightly oiled baking sheet. Divide spaghetti
equally among each slice. Top each one with remaining eggplant

slices, then cover with mozzarella and 1 or 2 slices tomato. Sprinkle with salt and pepper; bake in preheated 450°F oven for 10 minutes or until heated through and cheese is melted. Remove from oven and garnish with basil.

SERVES 4.

SPAGHETTI WITH UNCOOKED
GORGONZOLA SAUCE

*ere spaghetti combines beautifully—and so easily—
with velvety blue cheese and a sprinkling of crunchy
toasted pecans. Typically, three-quarters of a pound of
spaghetti would feed four people, but since this is quite rich, I
often serve smaller portions and so can satisfy up to six.*

¾ pound spaghetti
2 garlic cloves, finely chopped
2 tablespoons butter, at room temperature
½ pound Torta di Gorgonzola or Gorgonzola cheese,
   crumbled, at room temperature
   Lots of freshly ground black pepper
2 tablespoons freshly grated Parmesan cheese, plus
   extra for serving
⅓ cup pecan halves, lightly toasted, chopped

Cook pasta in large pot of boiling salted water until *al dente.*
Drain well. ❧ Meanwhile, place garlic, butter, Gorgonzola
cheese, pepper, and Parmesan cheese in large bowl. Add drained
pasta, toss until combined, and transfer to warmed dinner plates.
Garnish with pecans and serve with extra Parmesan cheese.

SERVES 4 TO 6.

SPAGHETTI LASAGNE

*n*ot fancy, that is true, but a deliciously satisfying and
exceedingly simple rendition of lasagne made with
spaghetti. I add a generous amount of Tabasco for lots
of flavor and a bit of heat, but by all means adjust the hot sauce
to your own taste.

¾ pound spaghetti, broken in half
2 large garlic cloves
1 can (28 ounces) tomatoes, undrained
1 tablespoon dried basil
1 teaspoon sugar
2 teaspoons Tabasco sauce
½ teaspoon salt
   Freshly ground black pepper
¾ pound Cheddar cheese, coarsely grated
4 tablespoons freshly grated Parmesan cheese

Cook pasta in large pot of boiling salted water until *al dente*; drain
well. ∽ Meanwhile, chop garlic in food processor. Add tomatoes
and purée. Blend in basil, sugar, Tabasco, salt, and pepper. ∽
Layer half the spaghetti in 8- x 8- x 2½-inch baking dish. Pour
half the sauce over pasta, then sprinkle with half the Cheddar and
2 tablespoons Parmesan cheese. Repeat once more in same order.
Bake in preheated 400°F oven for 30 minutes or until bubbly and
cheese is golden.

SERVES 4.

SUMMER SPAGHETTI

O ne of the lightest, freshest-tasting spaghetti sauces,
this dish reminds me of summer—no matter what
the season.

½ pound spaghetti or capellini
¼ cup olive oil
 2 large garlic cloves, finely chopped
¼ teaspoon hot red pepper flakes
 1 sweet yellow pepper, seeded, cut into julienne
 1 sweet red pepper, seeded, cut into julienne
 2 large ripe plum tomatoes, seeded, cut into julienne
 1 medium zucchini (½ pound), unpeeled, cut into
    julienne
½ teaspoon salt
    Freshly ground black pepper
 2 tablespoons drained tiny capers
½ cup chopped fresh basil or flat-leaf parsley
¼ cup freshly grated Parmesan cheese, plus extra
    for serving

Cook pasta in large pot of boiling salted water until *al dente*. ∾
Meanwhile, about 2 minutes after pasta has begun cooking, heat
olive oil in large nonstick skillet over medium-high heat. Add
garlic, red pepper flakes, sweet yellow and red peppers, tomatoes,
and zucchini and cook for 2 minutes or just until vegetables are
tender. ∾ Drain pasta well and add to vegetables in skillet.
Sprinkle with salt, pepper, capers, basil, and cheese; toss until
combined. Serve with extra cheese and pass the peppermill.

SERVES 2 TO 4.

SPAGHETTI COOKED IN
SPAGHETTI SAUCE

novel method of cooking spaghetti, the raw pasta is cooked right in the tomato sauce! The starch from the pasta thickens the sauce, and the sauce in turn permeates the pasta. To make it, you need extra-thin spaghetti such as vermicelli.

  2 tablespoons olive oil
  6 large garlic cloves, chopped
  1 can (28 ounces) tomatoes, undrained
1⅓ cups water
  ⅓ cup French dry white vermouth
  ¾ cup coarsely chopped fresh basil or flat-leaf parsley
  1 teaspoon sugar
    Salt and freshly ground black pepper
  ¼ teaspoon cayenne, or to taste
  6 ounces vermicelli
    Freshly grated Parmesan cheese

Heat oil in large nonstick or nonreactive skillet over medium-high heat. Add garlic and cook for 1 minute or until tender. Add tomatoes, crushing them with wooden spoon, then stir in water, vermouth, basil, sugar, salt, pepper, and cayenne; bring to a boil (maintain medium-high heat throughout cooking). Add pasta, stirring gently and fairly constantly to prevent pasta from sticking together. Cook for 8 minutes or until pasta is *al dente*. Serve at once with cheese.

SERVES 2 TO 3.

SPAGHETTI WITH ROASTED
TOMATOES

*r*oasting tomatoes in the oven gives them a remarkable, almost grilled flavor. They're perfectly delectable tossed with spaghetti, and a breeze to prepare, too. Ripe, full-flavored large-size plum tomatoes are essential.

2 pounds ripe plum tomatoes, cut lengthwise into
¼-inch thick slices
3 large garlic cloves, finely chopped
⅓ cup olive oil
1 tablespoon dried basil
1 teaspoon sugar
1 teaspoon Tabasco sauce
Salt and freshly ground black pepper
¼ cup freshly grated Parmesan cheese, plus extra
for serving
¾ pound spaghetti

Preheat oven to 450°F; adjust oven rack to highest shelf. ❧ Gently combine tomatoes with garlic, oil, basil, sugar, Tabasco sauce, salt, pepper, and cheese in large bowl. Arrange tomato mixture in single layer on large, low-sided (or tomatoes will steam) nonstick or nonreactive baking sheet. Bake for 30 minutes or until tomatoes are tender and edges have charred. ❧ Cook pasta in large pot of boiling salted water until *al dente.* Drain well and immediately toss with tomato mixture in large serving bowl. Serve with extra cheese and pass the peppermill.

SERVES 4.

photo overleaf ☞

SPAGHETTI WITH SPICY
TOMATO SALSA

P asta with Mexican salsa is simply sublime—you may never serve salsa with corn chips again! Ripe, full-flavored cherry tomatoes and fresh coriander (cilantro) are essential. The salsa must be freshly prepared, and immediately tossed with al dente spaghetti.

2 large garlic cloves
¼ cup coarsely chopped red onion
1 pound ripe cherry tomatoes
¼ cup pickled sliced jalapeños
1 teaspoon dried oregano
½ teaspoon salt
　Freshly ground black pepper
¼ cup olive oil
½ cup fresh coriander leaves, chopped, plus extra
　for garnish
½ pound spaghetti
　Freshly grated Parmesan cheese

Chop garlic in food processor. Add onion and process until finely diced. Add tomatoes and chiles and chop—do not purée. Transfer mixture to footed strainer and set in sink for 4 minutes to drain. Place in large serving bowl and stir in oregano, salt, pepper, oil, and coriander. ∾ Cook pasta in large pot of boiling salted water until *al dente*. Drain well, add to sauce in bowl, and toss until combined. Garnish with coriander and serve with cheese.

SERVES 2 TO 4.

THREE-MUSHROOM SPAGHETTI

*ost mushroom sauces call for heavy cream, so I
devised this marvelous, many-mushroomed version
with good-for-you olive oil instead. Brush mushrooms clean, don't
rinse them or they become soggy. If "exotic" mushrooms are
unavailable, don't substitute white button mushrooms, they just
don't make the grade.*

½ pound spaghetti
3 tablespoons olive oil
2 large garlic cloves, chopped
½ pound oyster mushrooms, stems removed,
    coarsely chopped
¼ pound shiitake mushrooms, stems removed,
    coarsely chopped
¼ pound chanterelles or cremini mushrooms,
    stems removed, coarsely chopped
    Salt and cracked or freshly ground black pepper
¼ cup chicken stock
¼ cup French dry white vermouth
    Freshly grated Parmesan cheese

Cook pasta in large pot of boiling salted water until *al dente*; drain
well. ❧ Meanwhile, heat oil in large nonstick skillet over
medium-high heat. Add garlic, mushrooms, salt, and cracked
pepper; cook for 2 minutes. Add stock and cook for a few
seconds; add vermouth and continue cooking several seconds
more or until about ¼ cup liquid remains. Add drained pasta to
skillet, toss until pasta absorbs liquid, and serve. Pass the cheese.

SERVES 2 TO 4.

SPAGHETTI WITH TOMATOES, OLIVES, FETA, AND MINT

*g*utsy Greek ingredients tossed with spaghetti is an appealing entrée that never fails to delight. Do not even think of using dried mint or canned domestic olives— the resulting dish will be bland and boring.

¼ cup olive oil
4 large garlic cloves, chopped
1 teaspoon dried oregano
¾ pound ripe cherry tomatoes, quartered
  Salt and freshly ground black pepper
½ cup Greek black olives (Kalamata), unpitted
½ pound spaghetti
1 cup crumbled feta cheese
¼ cup freshly grated Parmesan cheese, plus extra
  for serving
½ cup coarsely chopped fresh mint leaves
2 large green onions (green part only), chopped

Heat oil in large nonstick skillet over medium-high heat. Add garlic; cook for 1 minute or until tender. Add oregano, tomatoes, salt, and pepper and cook for 2 minutes or just until tomatoes are heated through; add olives and keep warm. ◔ Meanwhile, cook pasta in large pot of boiling salted water until *al dente*. Drain well; add to skillet. Add feta and Parmesan cheese, mint, and green onions; toss until combined and transfer to large serving bowl. Pass extra Parmesan cheese.

SERVES 2 TO 3.

photo overleaf ☞

SPAGHETTI WITH EGGPLANT

eggplant is one of my favorite vegetables, so I concocted this tomato-less eggplant sauce—tomatoes seem to sneak in and overpower most versions. The medley of garlic, chiles, red wine vinegar, and basil enhance—rather than mask—eggplant's voluptuous flavor. The sauce requires only minimal cooking, then it's set aside at room temperature to marinate—and that's it!

2 pounds eggplant, peeled, sliced into about ½- x
  1½-inch strips
1 tablespoon salt
⅓ cup olive oil
2 large garlic cloves, finely chopped
3 small dried red chiles, broken into small pieces,
  including seeds
3 tablespoons red wine vinegar
1 teaspoon dried basil
½ cup shredded fresh basil leaves
  Freshly ground black pepper
¾ pound spaghetti
  Freshly grated Parmesan cheese

Toss eggplant with salt in 2 large colanders; set aside for 45
minutes to drain, then thoroughly pat dry with paper towels. ⌘
Heat 2 tablespoons oil in large nonstick skillet over medium-high
heat. Add eggplant and cook for 4 minutes or until tender. ⌘
Combine eggplant with remaining oil, garlic, chiles, vinegar, dried
basil, ¼ cup fresh basil, and pepper in large serving bowl; set
aside for 1 to 2 hours—no longer—to allow flavors to blend.
⌘ Cook pasta in large pot of boiling salted water until *al dente*.
Drain well and immediately add to eggplant mixture. Sprinkle
with remaining basil and toss until combined. Serve with cheese
and pass the peppermill.

SERVES 4 TO 6.

SPAGHETTI WITH SHRIMP
AND TOMATOES

b *oth light and easy, this harmony of spaghetti, sweet-tasting shrimp, ripe cherry tomatoes, fresh herbs, and lemon zest is—without question—symphonically superb!*

¼ cup olive oil
4 large garlic cloves, chopped
½ teaspoon hot red pepper flakes
1 teaspoon dried oregano
1 teaspoon dried basil
1 pound raw medium shrimp, peeled, deveined
¾ pound ripe cherry tomatoes, quartered
  Salt and freshly ground black pepper
½ pound spaghetti
¼ cup freshly grated Parmesan cheese, plus extra
  for serving
¼ cup chopped fresh flat-leaf parsley
¼ cup chopped fresh basil leaves
  Grated zest of 1 medium lemon

Heat oil in large nonstick skillet over medium-high heat. Add garlic, red pepper flakes, oregano, dried basil, and shrimp; cook for 2 minutes or just until shrimp are cooked through. Add tomatoes, salt, and pepper and cook for 2 minutes or just until tomatoes are heated through; keep warm. ❧ Meanwhile, cook pasta in large pot of boiling salted water until *al dente*. Drain well and add to sauce in skillet. Add cheese, parsley, basil, and lemon zest; toss until combined. Serve with extra cheese.

SERVES 2 TO 4.

SPAGHETTI WITH INTENSELY-FLAVORED TOMATO SAUCE

enriching canned tomatoes with summery sun-dried tomatoes makes the most wonderful, intensely-flavored tomato sauce. A great sauce to serve in the wintertime— or anytime—when vine-ripened tomatoes are not available.

- 1 tablespoon olive oil
- 2 tablespoons sun-dried-tomato oil
- 4 large garlic cloves, chopped
- 1 medium-small onion, chopped
- 1 can (28 ounces) tomatoes, undrained
- 1 cup sun-dried tomatoes in oil, drained, chopped
- ¼ cup French dry white vermouth
  Freshly ground black pepper
- ¾ pound spaghetti
  Chopped flat-leaf parsley for garnish
  Freshly grated Parmesan cheese

Heat olive and sun-dried tomato oils in large nonstick or nonreactive skillet over medium-high heat. Add garlic and onion and cook for 2 minutes or until tender. Add tomatoes, crushing them with wooden spoon, then stir in sun-dried tomatoes, vermouth, and pepper. Cook for 20 minutes, stirring occasionally, or until slightly thickened. Cook pasta in large pot of boiling salted water until *al dente*. Drain well, add to sauce in skillet, and toss to combine. Transfer to large serving bowl, garnish with parsley, and serve with cheese.

SERVES 4.

SPAGHETTI WITH UNCOOKED
SUN-DRIED TOMATO SAUCE

ncomplicated and quite sensational, this savory sauce features an abundance of sweet sun-dried tomatoes (use only bright red ones, please) and fragrant basil. There's nothing more to it than whirling up the sauce in your food processor and tossing it with cooked spaghetti. The sauce may be done in advance.

3 large garlic cloves
1¾ cups sun-dried tomatoes in oil, well drained
¼ cup olive oil
2 tablespoons sun-dried-tomato oil
¾ pound spaghetti
½ cup shredded fresh basil leaves, plus extra
    for garnish
¼ cup freshly grated Parmesan cheese, plus extra
    for serving
    Freshly ground black pepper

Finely chop garlic in food processor. Add sun-dried tomatoes and olive and sun-dried tomato oils; coarsely chop—not to a paste. Transfer mixture to large serving bowl and set aside until serving—no longer than 4 hours. ❧ Cook pasta in large pot of boiling salted water until *al dente*. Drain well and add to sun-dried-tomato mixture; toss until combined. Sprinkle with basil, cheese, and pepper and toss again; garnish with basil. Serve with extra cheese and pass the peppermill.

SERVES 4 TO 6.

SPAGHETTI WITH BLACK OLIVES, ORANGE ZEST, AND BASIL

Z *ippy with the invigorating flavors of olives, garlic,*
orange zest, and fresh basil—here, Greek
Kalamata olives are vital: canned domestic olives don't pack
enough punch. This idea evolved from a recipe in my book,
All the Best Pasta Sauces.

¼ cup olive oil
2 large garlic cloves, chopped
   Grated zest of 1 medium-large orange
¾ cup Greek black olives (Kalamata), pitted,
   coarsely chopped
½ pound vermicelli
   Salt and freshly ground black pepper
½ cup coarsely shredded fresh basil leaves
2 tablespoons freshly grated Parmesan cheese, plus
   extra for serving

Heat oil in large nonstick skillet over medium-high heat. Add
garlic and cook for 30 seconds or until tender. Add orange zest
and olives; keep warm. ❧ Meanwhile, cook pasta in large pot of
boiling salted water until *al dente*. Drain well and add to olive
mixture. Sprinkle with salt, pepper, basil, and cheese; toss until
combined. Serve with extra cheese and pass the peppermill.

SERVES 3 TO 4.

SPAGHETTI WITH TUNA SAUCE

uickly prepared using staples—canned tuna and tomatoes—that everyone usually has on hand, this surprisingly tasty supper is a cinch in a crunch.

1 tablespoon olive oil
4 large garlic cloves, chopped
¼ teaspoon hot red pepper flakes
1 can (28 ounces) tomatoes, undrained
   Salt and freshly ground black pepper
1 can (7 ounces) chunk or solid white tuna
   (not flaked), drained
¼ cup chopped fresh flat-leaf parsley
1 tablespoon butter
2 tablespoons drained capers (optional)
¾ pound spaghetti
   Freshly grated Parmesan cheese

Heat oil in large nonstick or nonreactive skillet over medium-high heat. Add garlic and red pepper flakes; cook for 1 minute or until tender. Add tomatoes, crushing them with wooden spoon, salt, and pepper. Simmer for 20 minutes or until slightly thickened. Add tuna, breaking it into bite-size pieces, parsley, butter, and capers if desired; keep warm. ❧ Cook pasta in large pot of boiling salted water until *al dente*. Drain well and add to sauce in skillet; toss until combined. Serve with cheese and pass the peppermill.

SERVES 4.

SPAGHETTI WITH TOMATOES, OLIVES, AND CAPERS

t *his seductive amalgam of tomatoes, garlic, capers, black olives, and hot red pepper flakes dresses up spaghetti in the most delightfully gutsy way.*

2 tablespoons olive oil
6 large garlic cloves, chopped
¼ teaspoon hot red pepper flakes
1 can (28 ounces) tomatoes, undrained
1 teaspoon dried basil or oregano
  Freshly ground black pepper
1 cup Greek black olives (Kalamata), unpitted, or pitted and halved
2 tablespoons drained large capers
¾ pound vermicelli or spaghettini
¾ cup coarsely chopped fresh flat-leaf parsley, plus extra for garnish
  Freshly grated Parmesan cheese

Heat oil in large nonstick or nonreactive skillet over medium-high heat. Add garlic and red pepper flakes; cook for 1 minute or until tender. Stir in tomatoes, crushing them with wooden spoon, then add basil and pepper. Reduce heat to medium and cook for 20 minutes or until slightly thickened. Stir in olives and capers; keep warm. ❧ Cook pasta in large pot of boiling salted water until *al dente.* Drain well and add to sauce in skillet. Add parsley, toss to combine, and transfer to large serving bowl. Garnish with parsley. Serve with cheese and pass the peppermill.

SERVES 4.

SPAGHETTI PACKAGES

*b**aking spaghetti in parchment-paper or aluminum-foil
packages is an unusual though classic method used to
trap moisture and concentrate flavor. You may prepare
the packages a few hours ahead. The final baking takes only
minutes. Feel free to try different spaghetti recipes in the packages.*

Spaghetti with Intensely-flavored Tomato Sauce
(page 53)
¼ cup chopped fresh flat-leaf parsley or basil

Prepare spaghetti, omitting cheese. ∾ Meanwhile, cut four to six
12- x 13-inch pieces of parchment paper or aluminum foil. ∾
Place an equal amount of pasta on one half of each piece of
paper, spooning over any excess sauce. Sprinkle each portion with
parsley. Fold over, then roll and crimp edges securely to seal. ∾
Preheat oven to 375°F. Place packages on baking sheet and bake
for 15 minutes or until heated through. Transfer to individual
plates, allowing each guest to open their own package.

SERVES 4 TO 6.

SPAGHETTI PUDDING

*V*ermicelli noodles—extra-thin spaghetti—are
transformed into a yummy, sweet pasta pudding much
like rice pudding. This comfy dish is a Jewish specialty,
but my concoction is devised with spaghetti instead of the
traditional egg noodles.

½ pound vermicelli, broken into thirds
2 large eggs
1 large egg yolk
½ cup sugar
1 cup sour cream
½ cup milk
½ cup (1 stick) butter, melted, cooled
1 teaspoon salt
¼ teaspoon ground cinnamon
⅛ teaspoon grated nutmeg
1 teaspoon vanilla
   Grated zest of 1 medium lemon
   Grated zest of 1 medium orange
½ cup golden raisins
½ cup currants
1 teaspoon sugar mixed with ¼ teaspoon ground
   cinnamon
   Heavy cream for serving

Preheat oven to 350°F. ∿ Cook pasta in large pot of boiling salted water until *al dente*; drain well. ∿ Meanwhile, whisk eggs, egg yolk, and sugar in medium bowl until combined. Add sour cream, milk, butter, salt, cinnamon, nutmeg, vanilla, lemon and orange zests; whisk until blended. Stir in raisins and currants. ∿ Stir pasta and egg mixture in lightly buttered 2-quart baking dish until thoroughly combined and raisins and currants are evenly distributed. Bake for 30 minutes; remove from oven and sprinkle with sugar-cinnamon mixture. Return to oven and bake another 15 minutes or just until set but still slightly moist in center; don't overcook. Serve warm or at room temperature drizzled with cream if desired.

SERVES 6 TO 8.

COOKBOOKS BY JOIE WARNER

Joie Warner's Spaghetti: America's Favorite Pasta
Joie Warner's Caesar Salads: America's Favorite Salad
Joie Warner's Apple Desserts: America's Favorite Fruit
All The Best Pasta Sauces
All The Best Pizzas
All The Best Salads
All The Best Muffins and Quick Breads
All The Best Mexican Meals
All The Best Chicken Dinners
All The Best Stir-Fries
All The Best Potatoes
All The Best Rice
All The Best Pasta Sauces II
All The Best Cookies
The New Complete Book of Chicken Wings
The Braun Hand Blender Cookbook
A Taste of Chinatown